Pretending to Be a
Normal Person
Day After Day
Is Exhausting

ISBN: 978-1-59842-870-4

Wonderful Wacky Women®
Inspiring•Uplifting•Empowering

is a trademark of Suzy and Al Toronto. Used under license.

▌ and Blue Mountain Press are registered in U.S. Patent and Trademark Office. Certain trademarks are used under license.

Printed in China.
First Printing: 2015

✖ This book is printed on recycled paper.

This book is printed on paper that has been specially produced to be acid free (neutral pH) and contains no groundwood or unbleached pulp. It conforms with the requirements of the American National Standards Institute, Inc., so as to ensure that this book will last and be enjoyed by future generations.

Blue Mountain Arts, Inc.
P.O. Box 4549, Boulder, Colorado 80306

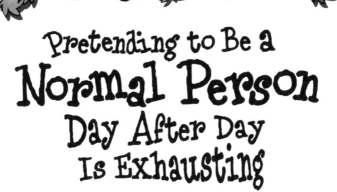

Pretending to Be a
Normal Person
Day After Day
Is Exhausting

Suzy Toronto

Blue Mountain Press™
Boulder, Colorado

William Shakespeare wrote,
"This above all: to thine own self be true."
Boy, did he nail it on the head!
A lot of us go through phases
where we think we have to be,
act, and look like everyone else
in order to fit in.
I tried it, and it didn't work.
Now I realize
God doesn't want an orchestra
of identical instruments
all playing the same tune,
so I let go of the status quo
and decided to just be me.

Besides, pretending to be a normal person
day after day is exhausting!

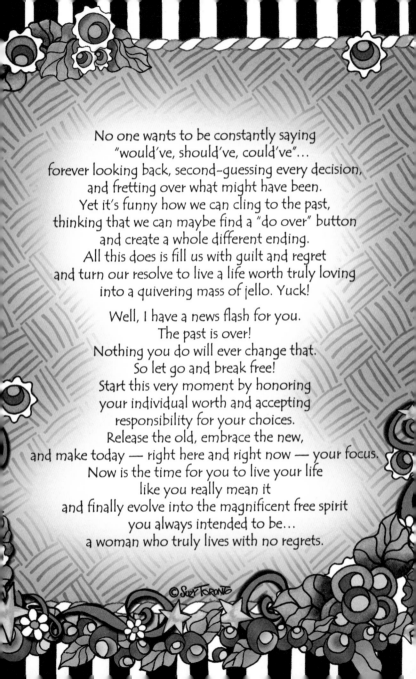

No one wants to be constantly saying
"would've, should've, could've"…
forever looking back, second-guessing every decision,
and fretting over what might have been.
Yet it's funny how we can cling to the past,
thinking that we can maybe find a "do over" button
and create a whole different ending.
All this does is fill us with guilt and regret
and turn our resolve to live a life worth truly loving
into a quivering mass of jello. Yuck!

Well, I have a news flash for you.
The past is over!
Nothing you do will ever change that.
So let go and break free!
Start this very moment by honoring
your individual worth and accepting
responsibility for your choices.
Release the old, embrace the new,
and make today — right here and right now — your focus.
Now is the time for you to live your life
like you really mean it
and finally evolve into the magnificent free spirit
you always intended to be…
a woman who truly lives with no regrets.

©Suzy Toronto

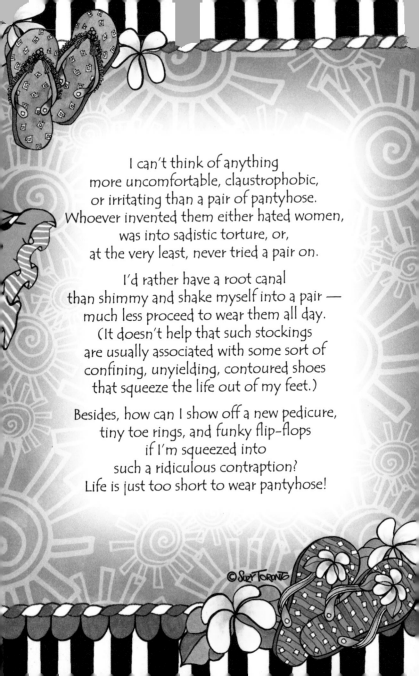

I can't think of anything
more uncomfortable, claustrophobic,
or irritating than a pair of pantyhose.
Whoever invented them either hated women,
was into sadistic torture, or,
at the very least, never tried a pair on.

I'd rather have a root canal
than shimmy and shake myself into a pair —
much less proceed to wear them all day.
(It doesn't help that such stockings
are usually associated with some sort of
confining, unyielding, contoured shoes
that squeeze the life out of my feet.)

Besides, how can I show off a new pedicure,
tiny toe rings, and funky flip-flops
if I'm squeezed into
such a ridiculous contraption?
Life is just too short to wear pantyhose!

© Suzy Toronto

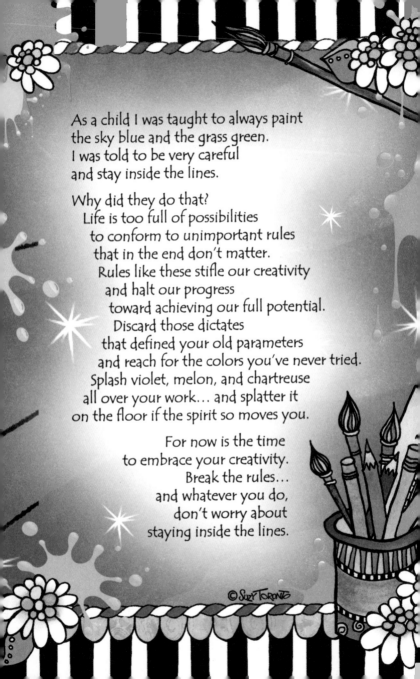

As a child I was taught to always paint
the sky blue and the grass green.
I was told to be very careful
and stay inside the lines.

Why did they do that?
    Life is too full of possibilities
        to conform to unimportant rules
            that in the end don't matter.
            Rules like these stifle our creativity
                and halt our progress
                    toward achieving our full potential.
                Discard those dictates
                    that defined your old parameters
                and reach for the colors you've never tried.
            Splash violet, melon, and chartreuse
        all over your work… and splatter it
on the floor if the spirit so moves you.

            For now is the time
            to embrace your creativity.
                Break the rules…
            and whatever you do,
                don't worry about
                staying inside the lines.

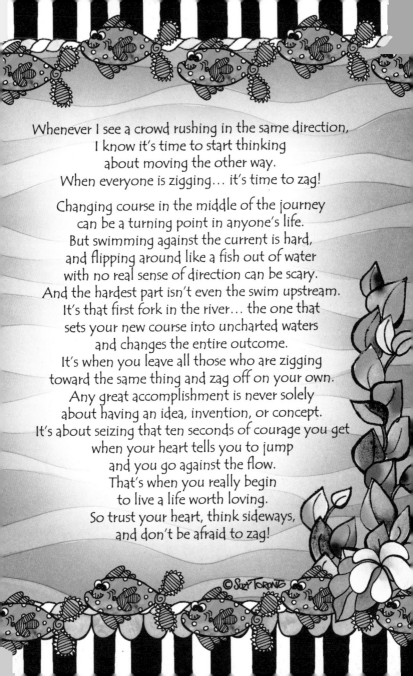

Whenever I see a crowd rushing in the same direction,
I know it's time to start thinking
about moving the other way.
When everyone is zigging... it's time to zag!

Changing course in the middle of the journey
can be a turning point in anyone's life.
But swimming against the current is hard,
and flipping around like a fish out of water
with no real sense of direction can be scary.
And the hardest part isn't even the swim upstream.
It's that first fork in the river... the one that
sets your new course into uncharted waters
and changes the entire outcome.
It's when you leave all those who are zigging
toward the same thing and zag off on your own.
Any great accomplishment is never solely
about having an idea, invention, or concept.
It's about seizing that ten seconds of courage you get
when your heart tells you to jump
and you go against the flow.
That's when you really begin
to live a life worth loving.
So trust your heart, think sideways,
and don't be afraid to zag!

© Suzy Toronto

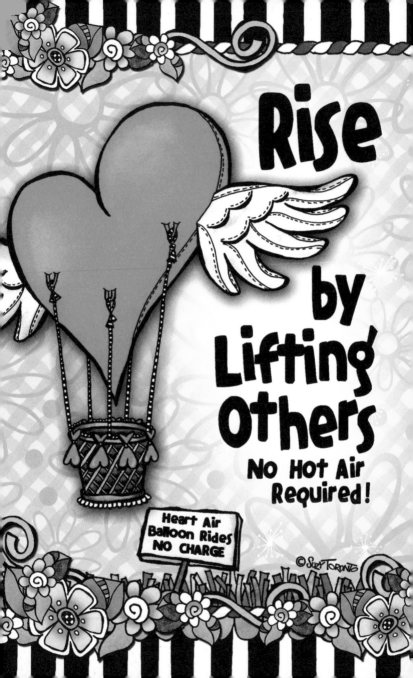

Everyone wants to get ahead in this world,
but it's hard when people go about it in thoughtless ways.
They puff themselves up with hot air, seek attention and praise,
and end up stepping on whomever they can to get higher.
Many of us know what that feels like —
been there! done that! — and it's really not that much fun.

The fact is that the real rise to the top
is a lot easier than it sounds.
Just let go of the idea that you need to climb
somewhere or something, and concentrate
on lifting and inspiring others along their journey.
When you stop focusing on yourself,
you end up finding extraordinary joy
in watching others' dreams take flight.

And here's the best part.
In the process, they become
the "wind beneath our wings."
We effortlessly float to the top
and find ourselves soaring higher than ever before.
The ride is a blast, and the view is amazing.
So inspire, uplift, and empower others.
It is the secret to true and lasting greatness.

In our effort to masquerade as people who really have our acts together, goofs, blunders, and faux pas often slip out. Sometimes these missteps are so unforgettable that they start to take on a life of their own. We get our feet stuck so far in our mouths or our skirts flung up so high over our heads that the spectacle is simply hard to miss.

This is where laughing at ourselves becomes a lifesaving virtue... because when we embrace our mistakes and make the best of the situation, we can just move on. After all, if there is going to be a big, goofy elephant in the room, you might as well introduce her!

So next time your
   inner "goofball" slips out,
        muster up all the wild energy
            you possess,
      throw your arms in the air,
   and give the world
a cross-eyed smile!

After all, we may do foolish things...
      but at least we do them
          with enthusiasm!

© Suzy Toronto

THERE ARE NO LIMITS TO THE SILLY THINGS I CAN ACCOMPLISH WHEN I'M SUPPOSED TO BE DOING SOMETHING ELSE

Where does it say in the book of life that absolutely everything we do has to be productive, on task, and worthy of a submission to the book of world records? Sometimes I think we get so wrapped up in accomplishing everything on our list that we forget the tremendous peace and solace we find in the simple things that give our bodies and minds a rest.

We get so wrapped up in the glorification
of busyness — becoming slaves to deadlines
and electronic day planners — that we forget
to "pencil in" some time for ourselves.

The truth is that doing it all and being it all is exhausting!
And, strangely enough, the endless scramble ends up
making us less productive than if we just slowed down
and allowed ourselves to do the things that
give our lives joy, fulfillment, and real meaning.

So... in the midst of our busy schedules,
our overcrowded calendars, and our endless flow charts,
let's get off the fast track, scratch the electronic lists,
and instead "ink in" some time to breathe... to giggle...
and to master the art of just doing nothing.
I'm pretty sure we'll find there are no limits to
the silly things we can accomplish when we're
supposed to be doing something else!
So let's say YES to a renewed sense
of whimsy and wacky with a
few hours of transformative,
unscheduled fun.

© Suzy Toronto

BECOMING AN ADULT IS the DUMBeST Thing I EVER DiD

Like most young people, I couldn't wait to come of age, become free to make my own choices and decisions about my life, and be a real, certified grownup. I wanted, wished, and waited with anticipation for my birthday, so I could declare to the world that I was officially an adult. But you know what? Becoming an adult is, without exception, the dumbest thing I ever did.

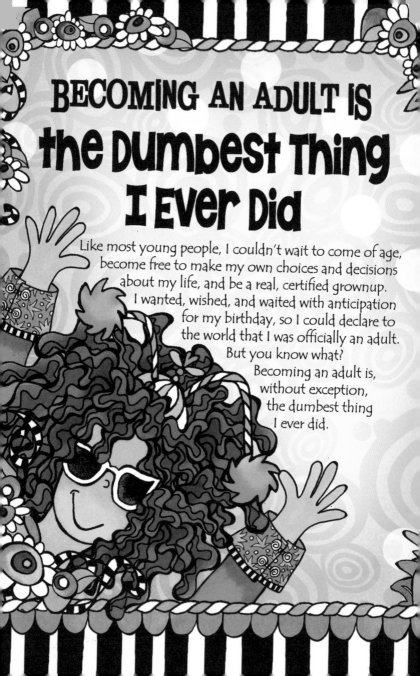

Now I wonder why I was in such a hurry.
Why did I think being responsible for everyone
and everything in the known universe was something
I needed to do? Why did I think that leaving behind
the carefree days of my youth in exchange for having
to act like an adult was going to be so fabulous?
I know that growing old is mandatory —
but growing up is not. In fact, I think
it's a trap to be avoided at all costs!

After giving it a lot of thought, I've decided
that being an adult is just not working for me.
But maybe, just maybe, it's not too late!
Here's my plan: From now on I'm going to stop
ignoring my inner child and embrace all things "kid."
I'm going to live, love, give, and play with the vibrant
passion, spunk, and spontaneity we all once had.
So be warned — the kid in me is coming out!

And if you feel the urge to give me milk and cookies,
wipe my face, and put me down for a nap,
I'm good with that too.
'Cause when it comes to childhood,
I'm hitting the "do over" button!
Wanna play?

© Suzy Toronto

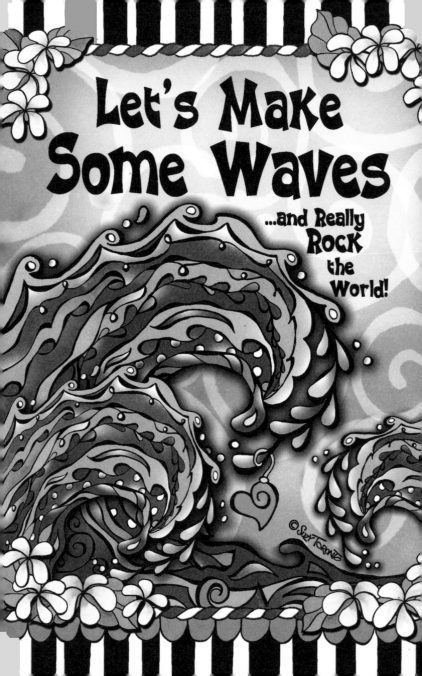

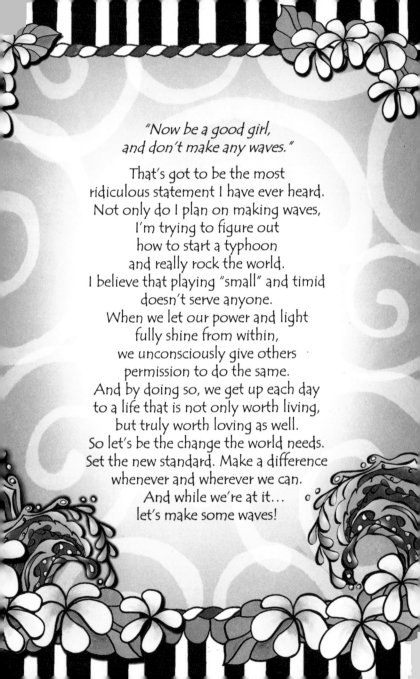

"Now be a good girl,
and don't make any waves."

That's got to be the most
ridiculous statement I have ever heard.
Not only do I plan on making waves,
I'm trying to figure out
how to start a typhoon
and really rock the world.
I believe that playing "small" and timid
doesn't serve anyone.
When we let our power and light
fully shine from within,
we unconsciously give others
permission to do the same.
And by doing so, we get up each day
to a life that is not only worth living,
but truly worth loving as well.
So let's be the change the world needs.
Set the new standard. Make a difference
whenever and wherever we can.
And while we're at it…
let's make some waves!

Some ideas sound logical
right from the start.
The wheel and fire were obviously
great concepts from the get-go.

But I wonder who first watched a chicken
lay an egg and said, "Hey, let's eat that."
That was probably met with some skeptical eyes.
At the time, no one had visions
of fluffy chiffons, lofty meringues,
yummy omelets, or delicate soufflés.

New ideas always encounter
criticism and opposition.
And most inventions begin
in somebody's basement
by one man or woman with a vision.
The key is to believe in yourself
and persevere.

So trust your crazy ideas.
They could change the world!

© Suzy Toronto

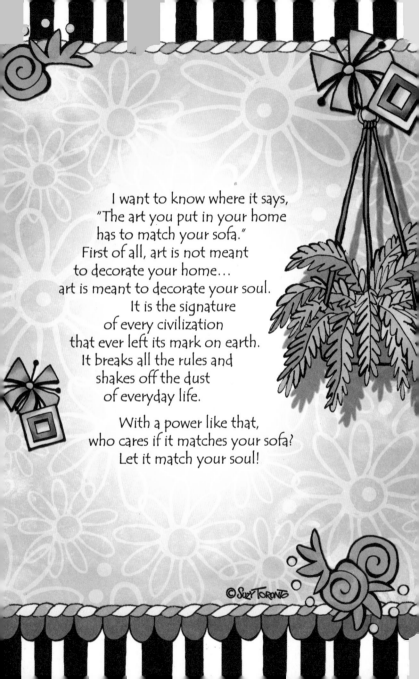

I want to know where it says,
"The art you put in your home
has to match your sofa."
First of all, art is not meant
to decorate your home...
art is meant to decorate your soul.
It is the signature
of every civilization
that ever left its mark on earth.
It breaks all the rules and
shakes off the dust
of everyday life.

With a power like that,
who cares if it matches your sofa?
Let it match your soul!

©Suzy Toronto

An Invisible Crown

Don't leave home without it!

Some of us are just born with glitter in our veins.
But, as boring as it is, there really are times
when we have to pretend to be normal,
no matter how exhausting it is.
(Sometimes we just have to conform!)

And even though I vow to never let anyone dull
my sparkle, some days it's just easier to put on
my invisible crown and head out the door.
I know it's there… even if no one else can see it.
As it perches atop my head, slightly askew,
it empowers me to glitter, sparkle, and shine
at the most wonderfully random times.
Sometimes I even use the secret button
right behind my ear that,
unbeknownst to everyone around me,
causes my crown to blink wildly
and play my theme song so loud
it drowns out everyone
and everything around me.
Of course, it's at a decibel that only
other wonderful, wacky women can hear.
But hey, that works for me!

So don't despair if occasionally
you need to pretend to be normal.
Just put on your invisible crown,
and keep your sparkle shining bright.

© Suzy Toronto

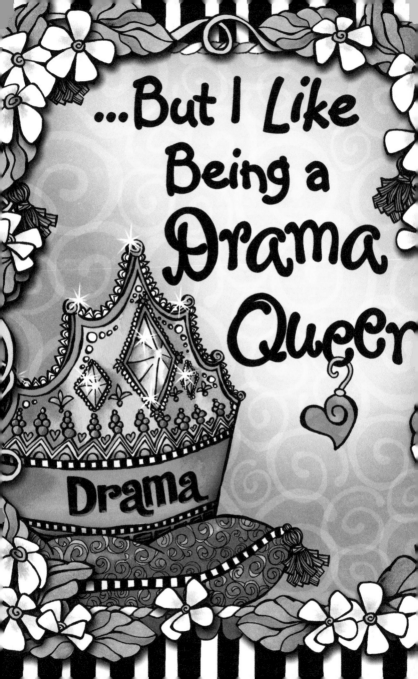

More than once, someone has rolled their eyes at me
and told me to quit being such a drama queen.

Instead of this stopping me in my tracks,
that one short sentence makes me want to seize
a can of spray adhesive with one hand
and a jar of glitter with the other and say,
"You're missing the whole point!"
and then cover them
with a lavish coat of sticky, iridescent bling.

But instead, I take a deep breath and say a silent prayer.
I pray for the strength that I will never, ever listen
to anyone who tells me to stop being myself.
I then vow to forever embrace the drama,
to breathe in the spark of passion that lights
a fire in my soul, and to always surround myself
with the wild energy that makes my heart tingle.

You know it, I know it:
sometimes we wonderful, wacky women
need to empower our inner drama queens
to help us create the excitement, passion, and fun
that truly make our lives worth loving…
no matter how many eyes are rolled along the way.

So stage your royal scene.
Script out your passionate performance.
And wear that crown with pride!

©Suzy Toronto

How old are you?
Personally, at this moment,
I have no idea how old I am.
I do remember a few milestone birthdays,
you know, 18, 21, 40…
but in my head, nothing has ever changed.
I keep wondering when
everyone is going to catch on
to the fact that for the last thirty years
I've been masquerading as an adult.

Perhaps we are, like the old saying goes,
"only as old as we feel."
In that case, I'll stay lost in my bewilderment…
because really, life is what we make it
and age is nothing but a state of mind.

©Suzy Toronto

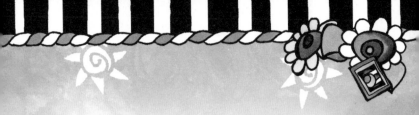

Sometimes life gives you a second chance.
Right in the middle of what seems like
a big bunch of muck,
a shiny brass ring appears
within your reach,
giving you a chance to start over.

Do not back away or question
whether it's your turn;
reach out with all the belief you've got.
Grab ahold of that ring for all it's worth
and never let go!

Miracles do happen,
and sometimes life does give you
a second chance.
So don't wait one second longer...
take it!

©Suzy Toronto

It's OK to Grab a Tiger by the Tail...

Even If You Don't Know What to Do Next!

Sometimes flying by the seat of your pants can get a little crazy — kind of like grabbing a tiger by the tail with no clue what to do next. Most of my life, I have thrown caution to the wind, jumped in with both feet, and learned to swim on the way up.

But things don't always go as planned. Many times the water was too deep or the wings I expected never appeared... sometimes both! But every time I dry myself off and get ready to try again, I don't focus on the misjudged leap or how I must have embarrassed myself beyond belief *that* time. Because the real tragedy would be if I had never even tried.

Reaching outside your comfort zone and taking a chance is worth any bumps and bruises you might get along the way. Once your adventure has begun, you'll find the trip is a kick, the possibilities are endless, and the journey is truly amazing.

So seriously, what are you waiting for? You have the power, knowledge, and drive inside you to perform extraordinary feats, but you have to be willing to risk it... you have to grab that tiger's tail and hang on for dear life as it swings you around.

All progress comes from daring to begin. So take a deep breath, and enjoy the ride!

© Suzy Toronto

☑ Are you willing to follow your dreams
with your arms flailing, hair flying,
and screaming at the top of your lungs?

☑ Are you a tad wacky…
and just shy of crazy?
Do you know how to have fun
and embrace every moment of your life
with passion and enthusiasm?

☑ Are you wonderful?
(No test here… let me answer for you.)
YES! Absolutely, positively, without a doubt.

Well, congratulations…
you passed the test.
You *are* a wild,
wonderful woman.
Welcome to the club, Sister…
Welcome to my world.

©Suzy Toronto

About the Author

So this is me… I'm a tad wacky and just shy of crazy. I'm fiftysomething and live in the sleepy village of Tangerine, Florida, with my husband, Al, and a big, goofy dog named Lucy. And because life wasn't crazy enough, my eightysomething-year-old parents live with us too. (In my home, the nuts don't fall far from the tree!) I eat far too much chocolate, and I drink sparkling water by the gallon. I practice yoga, ride a little red scooter, and go to the beach every chance I get. I have five grown children and over a dozen grandkids who love me as much as I adore them. I teach them to dip their French fries in their chocolate shakes and to make up any old words to the tunes they like. But most of all, I teach them to never, ever color inside the lines. This is the Wild Wacky Wonderful life I lead, and I wouldn't have it any other way. Welcome to my world!